Guest List

Guest List

Guest List

Guest List

Thoughts / Messages

With Love:_____

With Love:_____

With Love:_____

With Love:_____

Baby Shower

Thoughts / Messages

NAME:_____

NAME:_____

With Love:_____

With Love:_____

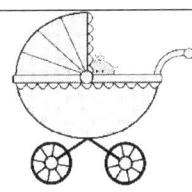

Baby Shower

Thoughts / Messages

With Love:_____

With Love:_____

With Love:_____

With Love:_____

 **Baby Shower**

Thoughts / Messages

With Love:_____

With Love:_____

With Love:_____

With Love:_____

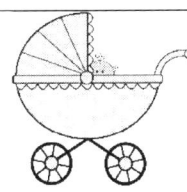

Baby Shower

Thoughts / Messages

With Love:_____

With Love:_____

With Love:_____

With Love:_____

Baby Shower

Thoughts / Messages

NAME:_____

NAME:_____

With Love:_____

With Love:_____

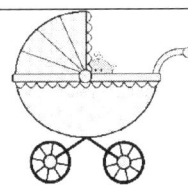

Baby Shower

Thoughts / Messages

With Love:_____

With Love:_____

With Love:_____

With Love:_____

Baby Shower

Thoughts / Messages

With Love:_____

With Love:_____

With Love:_____

With Love:_____

Baby Shower

Thoughts / Messages

With Love:_____

With Love:_____

With Love:_____

With Love:_____

Baby Shower

Thoughts / Messages

NAME:_____

NAME:_____

With Love:_____

With Love:_____

Baby Shower

Thoughts / Messages

With Love:_____

With Love:_____

With Love:_____

With Love:_____

Baby Shower

Thoughts / Messages

With Love:_____

With Love:_____

With Love:_____

With Love:_____

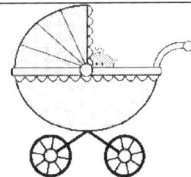

Baby Shower

Thoughts / Messages

With Love:_____

With Love:_____

With Love:_____

With Love:_____

Baby Shower

Thoughts / Messages

NAME:_____

NAME:_____

With Love:_____

With Love:_____

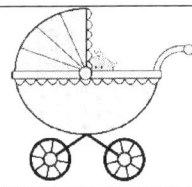

Baby Shower

Thoughts / Messages

With Love:_____

With Love:_____

With Love:_____

With Love:_____

Baby Shower

Thoughts / Messages

With Love:_____

With Love:_____

With Love:_____

With Love:_____

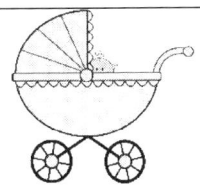

Baby Shower

Thoughts / Messages

With Love:_____

With Love:_____

With Love:_____

With Love:_____

Baby Shower

Thoughts / Messages

NAME:_____

NAME:_____

With Love:_____

With Love:_____

Baby Shower

Thoughts / Messages

With Love:_____

With Love:_____

With Love:_____

With Love:_____

Baby Shower

Thoughts / Messages

With Love:_____

With Love:_____

With Love:_____

With Love:_____

Baby Shower

Thoughts / Messages

With Love:_____

With Love:_____

With Love:_____

With Love:_____

Baby Shower

Thoughts / Messages

NAME:_____

NAME:_____

With Love:_____

With Love:_____

Baby Shower

Thoughts / Messages

With Love:_____

With Love:_____

With Love:_____

With Love:_____

Baby Shower

Thoughts / Messages

With Love:_____

With Love:_____

With Love:_____

With Love:_____

Baby Shower

Thoughts / Messages

With Love:_____

With Love:_____

With Love:_____

With Love:_____

Baby Shower

Thoughts / Messages

NAME:_____

NAME:_____

With Love:_____

With Love:_____

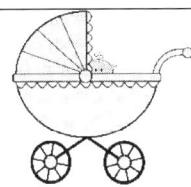

Baby Shower

Thoughts / Messages

With Love:_____

With Love:_____

With Love:_____

With Love:_____

Baby Shower

Thoughts / Messages

With Love:_____

With Love:_____

With Love:_____

With Love:_____

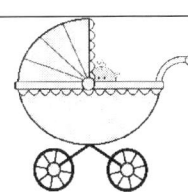

Baby Shower

Thoughts / Messages

With Love:_____

With Love:_____

With Love:_____

With Love:_____

Baby Shower

Thoughts / Messages

NAME:_____

NAME:_____

With Love:_____

With Love:_____

Baby Shower

Thoughts / Messages

With Love:_____

With Love:_____

With Love:_____

With Love:_____

Baby Shower

Thoughts / Messages

With Love:_____

With Love:_____

With Love:_____

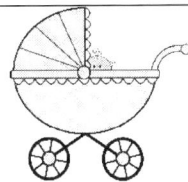

With Love:_____

Baby Shower

Thoughts / Messages

With Love:_____

With Love:_____

With Love:_____

With Love:_____

Baby Shower

Thoughts / Messages

NAME:_____

NAME:_____

With Love:_____

With Love:_____

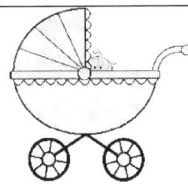

Baby Shower

Thoughts / Messages

With Love:_____

With Love:_____

With Love:_____

With Love:_____

Baby Shower

Thoughts / Messages

With Love:_____

With Love:_____

With Love:_____

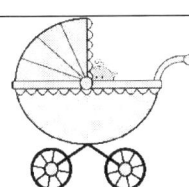

With Love:_____

Baby Shower

Thoughts / Messages

With Love:_____

With Love:_____

With Love:_____

With Love:_____

Baby Shower

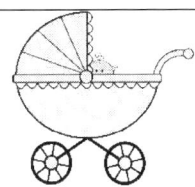

Thoughts / Messages

NAME:_____

NAME:_____

With Love:_____

With Love:_____

Baby Shower

Thoughts / Messages

With Love:_____

With Love:_____

With Love:_____

With Love:_____

Baby Shower

Thoughts / Messages

With Love:_____

With Love:_____

With Love:_____

With Love:_____

Baby Shower

Thoughts / Messages

With Love:_____

With Love:_____

With Love:_____

With Love:_____

Baby Shower

Thoughts / Messages

NAME:_____

NAME:_____

With Love:_____

With Love:_____

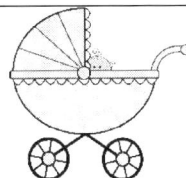

Baby Shower

Thoughts / Messages

With Love:_____

With Love:_____

With Love:_____

With Love:_____

Baby Shower

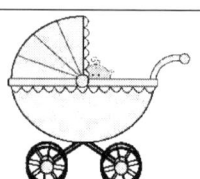

Thoughts / Messages

With Love:_____

With Love:_____

With Love:_____

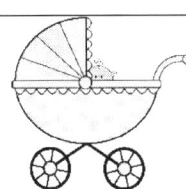

With Love:_____

Baby Shower

Thoughts / Messages

With Love:_____

With Love:_____

With Love:_____

With Love:_____

Baby Shower

Thoughts / Messages

NAME:_____

NAME:_____

With Love:_____

With Love:_____

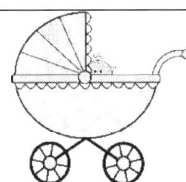

Baby Shower

Thoughts / Messages

With Love:_____

With Love:_____

With Love:_____

With Love:_____

Baby Shower

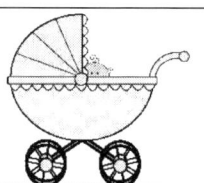

Thoughts / Messages

With Love:_____

With Love:_____

With Love:_____

With Love:_____

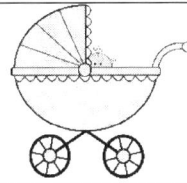

Baby Shower

Thoughts / Messages

With Love:_____

With Love:_____

With Love:_____

With Love:_____

Baby Shower

Thoughts / Messages

NAME:_____

NAME:_____

With Love:_____

With Love:_____

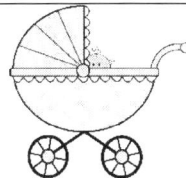

Baby Shower

Thoughts / Messages

With Love:_____

With Love:_____

With Love:_____

With Love:_____

Baby Shower

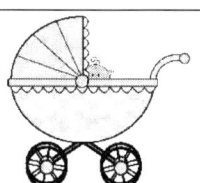

Thoughts / Messages

With Love:_____

With Love:_____

With Love:_____

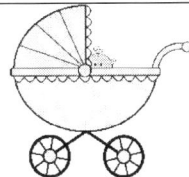

With Love:_____

Baby Shower

Thoughts / Messages

With Love:_____

With Love:_____

With Love:_____

With Love:_____

Baby Shower

Thoughts / Messages

NAME:_____

NAME:_____

With Love:_____

With Love:_____

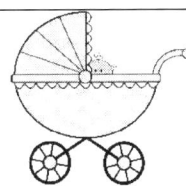

Baby Shower

Thoughts / Messages

With Love:_____

With Love:_____

With Love:_____

With Love:_____

Baby Shower

Thoughts / Messages

With Love:_____

With Love:_____

With Love:_____

With Love:_____

Baby Shower

Thoughts / Messages

With Love:_____

With Love:_____

With Love:_____

With Love:_____

Baby Shower

Thoughts / Messages

NAME:_____

NAME:_____

With Love:_____

With Love:_____

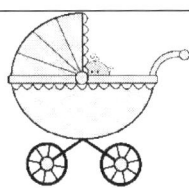

Baby Shower

Thoughts / Messages

With Love:_____

With Love:_____

With Love:_____

With Love:_____

Baby Shower

Thoughts / Messages

With Love:_____

With Love:_____

With Love:_____

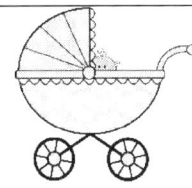

With Love:_____

Baby Shower

Thoughts / Messages

With Love:_____

With Love:_____

With Love:_____

With Love:_____

Baby Shower

Thoughts / Messages

NAME:_____

NAME:_____

With Love:_____

With Love:_____

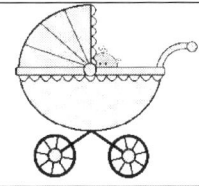

Baby Shower

Thoughts / Messages

With Love:_____

With Love:_____

With Love:_____

With Love:_____

Baby Shower

Thoughts / Messages

With Love:_____

With Love:_____

With Love:_____

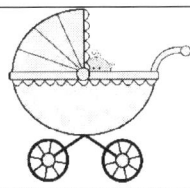

With Love:_____

Baby Shower

Thoughts / Messages

With Love:_____

With Love:_____

With Love:_____

With Love:_____

Baby Shower

Thoughts / Messages

NAME:_____

NAME:_____

With Love:_____

With Love:_____

Baby Shower

Thoughts / Messages

With Love:_____

With Love:_____

With Love:_____

With Love:_____

Baby Shower

Thoughts / Messages

With Love:_____

With Love:_____

With Love:_____

With Love:_____

Baby Shower

Thoughts / Messages

With Love:_____

With Love:_____

With Love:_____

With Love:_____

Baby Shower

Thoughts / Messages

NAME:_____

NAME:_____

With Love:_____

With Love:_____

Baby Shower

Thoughts / Messages

With Love:_____

With Love:_____

With Love:_____

With Love:_____

Baby Shower

Thoughts / Messages

With Love:_____

With Love:_____

With Love:_____

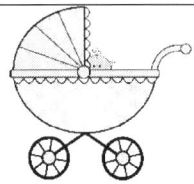

With Love:_____

Baby Shower

Thoughts / Messages

With Love:_____

With Love:_____

With Love:_____

With Love:_____

Baby Shower

Thoughts / Messages

NAME:_____

NAME:_____

With Love:_____

With Love:_____

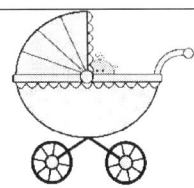

Baby Shower

Thoughts / Messages

With Love:_____

With Love:_____

With Love:_____

With Love:_____

Baby Shower

Thoughts / Messages

With Love:_____

With Love:_____

With Love:_____

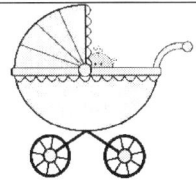

With Love:_____

Baby Shower

Thoughts / Messages

With Love:_____

With Love:_____

With Love:_____

With Love:_____

Baby Shower

Thoughts / Messages

NAME:_____

NAME:_____

With Love:_____

With Love:_____

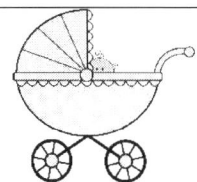

Baby Shower

Thoughts / Messages

With Love:_____

With Love:_____

With Love:_____

With Love:_____

Baby Shower

Thoughts / Messages

With Love:_____

With Love:_____

With Love:_____

With Love:_____

Baby Shower

Thoughts / Messages

With Love:_____

With Love:_____

With Love:_____

With Love:_____

Baby Shower

Thoughts / Messages

NAME:_____

NAME:_____

With Love:_____

With Love:_____

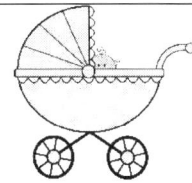

Baby Shower

Thoughts / Messages

With Love:_____

With Love:_____

With Love:_____

With Love:_____

Baby Shower

Thoughts / Messages

With Love:_____

With Love:_____

With Love:_____

With Love:_____

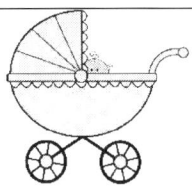

Baby Shower

GIFT LOG

DATE	GIFT DESCRIPTION	GIVEN BY	THANK YOU NOTICE SENT

GIFT LOG

DATE	GIFT DESCRIPTION	GIVEN BY	THANK YOU NOTICE SENT

GIFT LOG

DATE	GIFT DESCRIPTION	GIVEN BY	THANK YOU NOTICE SENT

GIFT LOG

DATE	GIFT DESCRIPTION	GIVEN BY	THANK YOU NOTICE SENT

GIFT LOG

DATE	GIFT DESCRIPTION	GIVEN BY	THANK YOU NOTICE SENT

GIFT LOG

DATE	GIFT DESCRIPTION	GIVEN BY	THANK YOU NOTICE SENT

GIFT LOG

DATE	GIFT DESCRIPTION	GIVEN BY	THANK YOU NOTICE SENT

GIFT LOG

DATE	GIFT DESCRIPTION	GIVEN BY	THANK YOU NOTICE SENT

GIFT LOG

DATE	GIFT DESCRIPTION	GIVEN BY	THANK YOU NOTICE SENT

GIFT LOG

DATE	GIFT DESCRIPTION	GIVEN BY	THANK YOU NOTICE SENT

GIFT LOG

DATE	GIFT DESCRIPTION	GIVEN BY	THANK YOU NOTICE SENT

Baby Shower Games

1) Mary had a little lamb, it's _____ was white as snow.

2) Baa, baa, black sheep, have you any _____?

3) Mary, Mary, quite _____, how does your garden grow?

4) Rub-a-dub-dub, three men in a tub, and how do you think _____ _____ _____?

5) Pat-a-cake, pat-a-cake, _____ _____!

6) Little Jack Horner, sat in a corner, eating his _____ pie;

7) Little Miss Muffet, sat on a tuffet, eating her _____ and _____.

8) Peter Piper picked a peck of _____ _____.

9) One, two, buckle my shoe, three four, _____ at the door.

10) Peter, Peter, pumpkin-eater, had a wife but couldn't _____ her.

11) Old Mother Hubbard, went to the _____.

12) There was an old woman, who lived in a _____.

13) Jack Sprat could eat no fat, his wife could eat no _____.

14) Hey diddle, diddle, the _____ and the fiddle.

15) Rock-a-bye baby, on the _____.

Answers

Here are the answers below to the questions. It is great to give the winner a baby shower small gift for participating. Read the answers that people have put out loud since you will have some funny ones.

1) fleece   2) wool 3) contrary   4) they got there   5) Baker's man

6) Christmas   7) curds, whey 8) pickled peppers   9) knock   10) keep

11) cupboard 12) shoe   13) lean   14) cat 15) treetop

To print out this game, turn on your printer, click here, when the checklist comes up, click the "File --> Print Option" in your browser).

Baby Shower Games

Baby shower games at your baby shower can be one of the most memorable experiences during the pre-baby events that will take place for the days to come. Part of making the experience successful is by thoughtful party planning and having fun baby shower games! Before starting the baby shower games, it is always good to go around the room first as an ice breaker and have everyone introduce themselves and how they know the Mother-To-Be. Below we have listed the most popular baby shower games to play during the baby shower:

1) Guess Mom's Tummy Size: (Materials- String or yarn and scissors) Have each woman pull the yarn to the size they believe would fit perfectly around the Mother-To-Be's center of her pregnant tummy. After everyone cuts their string, compare the results to the Mommy-To-Be's actual tummy. Give a prize to the woman who is the most close! This is a baby shower favorite.

2) Never say "Baby": (Materials- baby safety pins or another type of baby object you can place on a string for each woman at the party as well as string or yarn, enough for each woman to wear as a necklace). Have each woman place the necklace with the baby safety pins around her neck when she gets to the party. The rules for this baby shower game are given out at the beginning of the baby shower that whenever someone says the word "baby" during the shower, any woman who calls it out gets a pin from the other woman who stated the word. At the end of the baby shower, the woman with the most pins wins a prize.

3) How Many Baby Items Can You Name: (Materials- pad of paper and pen for each woman). Have each woman write down as many baby products as they can name (bottle, blanket, pacifier, etc) within 5 minutes. Sure it is easy at the beginning, but towards the last few minutes, the women will start racking their brains for more :) Give a prize to the woman who gets the most baby products named!

4) Who Can Make The Mother-To-Be's Baby: (Materials - Baby magazines, Scissors, Glue, Paper). Have the women group up into teams of 3 and give each 3 baby magazines. Have them cut out pieces of different baby qualities and put together a picture of what they think the Mother-To-Be's baby will look like. Have the Mother-To-Be pick which baby would possibly look like hers the best! Give prizes to the winning team! One of the top baby shower games!

5) Guess The Gerber's: (Materials - Gerber's infant food, pads of paper and pens). Take the labels off of the baby food jars and have the women at the baby shower guess the food (carrots, peas, sweet potato). Most fun to play up to 10 jars of different kinds of foods. If there is a tie, blindfold the women and have them taste one of the jars and guess the right flavor to win their prize.

6) Guess How Many Safety Pins: (Materials- Safety Pins and Jar). Pass around a jar full of baby safety pins. The one who guesses the closest wins a baby shower prize. A baby shower game favorite!

One of our visitors, Lynn, stated that she filled a clear plastic container (about 50 qt size with disposable diapers) all the same size (size 1) and had people guess how many diapers were in the container. Of course, container and contents go to mom since, as we all know, you can never have enough diapers. This baby shower game is very functional for the mommy-to-be!

You can also add cute clothes pins by getting a few packs and using them for the baby shower game, then spreading them around the tables as decorations!

7) How Well Do You Know Mommy-To-Be: (Materials- Pre-Printed Form and pen for each woman). Have each women guess what features she wants most on the baby from either her or her husband (Daddy-To-Be). An example of this idea is found below:

Attribute	Mommy	Daddy
Eyes	X	
Ears		X
Nose	X	
Legs		X
Hair	X	
Smile		X
Intelligence		X
Humor	X	
Other	X	

Select 25 attributes and ask everyone to fill in the form from what each woman feels the "mommy-to-be's" point of view" will be. After everyone checks off the list, have the mommy-to-be state her preference. The one with the most correct match to the Mommy-To-Be wins a prize. This is a great baby shower game!

8) Place The Baby On The Mommy: (Materials- Cutouts of a baby with tape and blindfold). Another one of our favorite baby shower games is the baby shower version of Pin The Tail on the Donkey. Blindfold each participant and then give them a paper baby to then approach the mom and place the baby as close to the tummy as possible. The one who gets closest to placing the paper baby on the pregnant tummy wins.

9) Bottle Races: (Materials- Baby bottles with Milk or alternate drink). Have each participant take a bottle filled with a liquid and suck the bottle as a baby would. The woman who drinks the most in an alloted time wins the baby shower gift. This baby shower game gets everyone laughing!

10) Baby Bingo: (Materials- Pens, Pre-Printed Bingo cards that use the numbers of how many people attend the baby shower) Prior to opening the baby shower gifts, number each gift on the box starting with one. If you know that 15 people will be attending your shower, pre-print bingo cards with numbers 1 through 15 and randomly place them on 15 cards. When the mommy-to-be's decides to open the presents, she grabs the present she wants to open and reads the number out loud. As soon as someone receives bingo, they win the baby shower game and the baby shower prize.

11) "B" is for Baby: (Materials paper and pens passed out to all the women). Each woman is told to write the babies Mom-To-Be and Father-To-Be's name on a paper going vertically down the page. Next to each letter of both names, create a word that is baby related or things that kids like. An example of using the names Kim and Dan:

K= kite   D=drool

I= ice cream   A=alphabet

M= mother   N=nap

The one who guesses the most words that are the same as the mother-to-be wins a prize.

12) Guess the baby item: (Materials- any baby products and blindfold). A bag of baby items are placed in front of the mother-to-be for her to take one item out at a time blindfolded and tell her baby shower guests what item she has in her hands. This is really fun baby shower game when you choose some crazy baby toys or products.

13) Finish the Baby Rhyme: (Materials- baby rhyme game or a book containing the rhymes). Have the host read out loud a part of the rhyme to be finished by the other women. Let's see how many Baby Shower Guests can finish the following Rhymes we have all grown up with:

1) Mary had a little lamb, it's _____ was white as snow.

2) Baa, baa, black sheep, have you any _____?

3) Mary, Mary, quite _____, how does your garden grow?

4) Rub-a-dub-dub, three men in a tub, and how do you think _____ _____ _____?

5) Pat-a-cake, pat-a-cake, _____ _____!

6) Little Jack Horner, sat in a corner, eating his _____ pie;

7) Little Miss Muffet, sat on a tuffet, eating her _____ and _____.

8) Peter Piper picked a peck of _____ _____.

9) One, two, buckle my shoe, three four, _____ at the door.

10) Peter, Peter, pumpkin-eater, had a wife but couldn't _____ her.

11) Old Mother Hubbard, went to the _____.

12) There was an old woman, who lived in a _____.

13) Jack Sprat could eat no fat, his wife could eat no _____.

14) Hey diddle, diddle, the _____ and the fiddle.

15) Rock-a-bye baby, on the _____.

Here are the answers below to the questions. It is great to give the winner a baby shower small gift for participating. Read the answers that people have put out loud since you will have some funny ones.

1) fleece   2) wool   3) contrary   4) they got there   5) Baker's man

6) Christmas   7) curds, whey   8) pickled peppers   9) knock   10) keep

11) cupboard   12) shoe   13) lean   14) cat   15) treetop

To print out this game, turn on your printer, click here, when the checklist comes up, click the "File --> Print Option" in your browser).

14) Guess the baby pictures: Ask for everyone's pictures prior to the baby shower. Have all the pictures in a collage and make lines for people to fill in who they think the babies are out of the girls at the baby shower. If most women don't know each other, just have the pictures of the mother, mother-in-law, sisters, and mommy-to-be. See how many

people guess right. You can make copies of the baby picture collage to see how many can guess right!

15) Baby Scrambler: Another fun baby shower game is to choose around 25 baby related items and scramble the spelling. For instance, pacifier can be changed to reiifpca. Have the women unscramble the words. The one who gets the most right in 5 min receives a baby shower prize.

Made in the USA
Lexington, KY
20 July 2019